FM 17-68
WAR DEPARTMENT FIELD MANUAL

M5 STUART LIGHT TANK CREW MANUAL
BY WAR DEPARTMENT

RESTRICTED Dissemination of restricted matter. —The information contained in restricted documents and the essential characteristics of restricted material may be given to any person known to be in the service of the United States and to persons of undoubted loyalty and discretion who are cooperating in Government work, but will not be communicated to the public or in the press except by authorized military public relations agencies. (See also par. 18b, AR 330-5, 28 Sep 1942.)

WAR DEPARTMENT • 24 MAY 1944
DECLASSIFIED

©2011 PERISCOPE FILM LLC
ALL RIGHTS RESERVED
ISBN #978-1-935700-80-7
WWW.PERISCOPEFILM.COM

FM 17-68
C 1

~~RESTRICTED~~

FIELD MANUAL

ARMORED

CREW DRILL, LIGHT TANK M5 SERIES

Changes ⎫   WAR DEPARTMENT,
No. 1 ⎭   Washington, 4 December 1944.

FM 17-68, 24 May 1944, is changed as follows:

5. OPERATION OF INTERPHONE AND RADIO.

* * * * *

a. M5 light tank.

* * * * *

(2) The tank commander depresses the switch on his microphone cord, and orders: CHECK INTERPHONE. NOTE: This command is * * * the interphone check.

* * * * *

(3) The **gunner,** bow gunner, and driver, in turn, **throw their radio-interphone switches to INTERPHONE**, depress their microphone switches, and report: **"Gunner check," "Bog check," "Driver check." Upon completion of their reports, they immediately return their switches to RADIO.** During this procedure, * * * the switch button.

* * * * *

(5) (Superseded). The RADIO-INT switches on all control boxes, except the tank commander's, must be set on RADIO. This is the normal position for interphone operation. The tank commander's switch will be set at INT most of the time; he will change it to RADIO only as he desires radio communication.

FIELD MANUAL

Except in an emergency, *no one but the tank commander* may operate the RADIO-INT switch on his control box. In an emergency, a member of the tank crew may communicate with the tank commander or another crew member by throwing his control box switch to INT; but this action will interrupt the tank commander's radio reception. It is the duty of the tank commander to monitor his radio receiver at all times except when speaking over the interphone or transmitting over the radio. He can monitor both the interphone and the radio receiver with his switch set at the INT position.

* * * * *

CREW DRILL, LIGHT TANK M5 SERIES

35. BEFORE OPERATION INSPECTION. Tank locked and covered with tarpaulin. All crew members check for tampering and damages. (NOTE: For training * * * * deficiencies as found).

PHASE B

Tank Commander	Gunner	Bow Gunner	Driver
*	*	*	*
*	*	Close engine compartment doors.	Auxiliary generator oil level.
		Notify Driver to turn on switch.	**Turn on master switch.**
	Report "Gunner ready."	Report "Bog ready."	Start generator; check operation.
Command REPORT.			Report "Driver ready."

PHASE C (Superseded)

Tank Commander	Gunner	Bow Gunner	Driver
Command PERFORM PHASE C.	Check the following: Oil in turret reservoir.		Start engines. Check instruments, warning lights, and siren.
Direct Driver to move tank forward 2 tank lengths.			

FIELD MANUAL

Tank Commander	Gunner	Bow Gunner	Driver
Walk ahead of tank; check condition of right track shoes and inside wedge nuts and connectors.	Oil can and stabilizer oil. All firing controls. Turn on turret master switch.	Walk behind tank; check condition of left track shoes and inside wedge nuts and connectors.	Drive tank slowly forward 2 tank lengths.
Check outer wedge nuts and connectors; watch action and check condition of support rollers, shoes, and tank suspension as tank moves to rear.	Check stabilizer operation, oil reservoir connections and pump.	Direct Driver to move to rear; tighten inside sprocket ring cap screws as exposed. Tighten outside cap screws.	Drive tank to rear as directed by Bog. Stop engines.
		Replace tools in bag; pass to Driver. Help Driver check lights.	Receive and stow tools. Check driving and blackout lights.
		Check machine gun tripod case for pintle and elevating mechanism. Install radio antenna. Replace tarpaulin on rear deck.	

4

AGO 154D

CREW DRILL, LIGHT TANK M5 SERIES

Pass rammer staff to Bog and cleaning rod to Gunner.	Receive and stow machine gun cleaning rod.	Receive and stow rammer staff.	Close hatch.
Mount to turret.	Check that Driver's and Bog's hatches are closed.	Take mounted post; close hatch.	
	Check manual elevation, operation of hand and power traverse, and turret lock.		
Help check recoil oil.	Check recoil cylinder oil.		
Connect break-away plugs.	Connect break-away plugs.	Connect break-away plugs.	Connect break-away plugs.
Command REPORT (interphone check).	Report "gunner ready."	Report "Bog ready."	Report "Driver ready."

NOTE: In later models of the Light Tank M5A1, there is an *emergency ignition switch* on the right side of the hull roof. This switch is left in the ON position except in emergencies, when it is used by the Tank Commander or other personnel within reach.

FIELD MANUAL

40. RADIO.

* * * * *

g. **Tubes** (Superseded.) Turn in defective tubes at the earliest opportunity.

* * * * *

[AG 300.7 (31 Oct 44).]

BY ORDER OF THE SECRETARY OF WAR:

OFFICIAL: G. C. MARSHALL
J. A. ULIO *Chief of Staff*
Major General
The Adjutant General

DISTRIBUTION:
AAF(10); AGF (10); ASF (10); **T of Opns** (5); **Arm & Sv Bd** (2); Def C (5); Tech Sv (2); SvC (10); HD (5); PC&S (1); Gen & Sp Sv Sch (50) except Armd Sch (500); USMA (2); ROTC (1); A (10); CHQ (10); D (2) except D 2, 7, 17 (10); R 2, 17 (10); SBn 2, 17 (10); Bn 2, 17 (5); AF (2).
T/O & E: 17-2 (5); 17-17 (20); 17-20-1 (5).
For explanation of symbols, see FM 21-6.

WAR DEPARTMENT FIELD MANUAL
FM 17-68
This manual supersedes FM 17-68, 8 June 1943

ARMORED

CREW DRILL

LIGHT TANK M5 SERIES

WAR DEPARTMENT · 24 MAY 1944

RESTRICTED *DISSEMINATION OF RESTRICTED MATTER.*—The Information contained in restricted documents and the essential characteristics of restricted material may be given to any person known to be in the service of the United States and to persons of undoubted loyalty and discretion who are cooperating in Government work, but will not be communicated to the public or to the press except by authorized military public relations agencies. (See also par. 23b, AR 380-5, 15 Mar 1944.)

United States Government Printing Office
Washington 1944

WAR DEPARTMENT,
WASHINGTON 25, D. C., 24 May 1944.

FM 17-68, Armored Field Manual, Crew Drill, Light Tank M5 Series, is published for the information and guidance of all concerned.

[A. G. 300.7 (24 May 44).]

BY ORDER OF THE SECRETARY OF WAR:

G. C. MARSHALL,
Chief of Staff.

OFFICIAL:

J. A. ULIO,
Major General.
The Adjutant General.

DISTRIBUTION:

As prescribed in paragraph 9a, FM 21-6, except Armd Sch (500); D 2, 7, 17 (10); R, 17 (10); Bn 2, 17 (5); IC 17 (5), (20).

IC 17: T/O & E, Hq Co, Armd Div; 17-20-1, Hq and Hq Co, Combat Comd, Armd Div (5); 17-17, Light Tk Co, Tank Bn and Light Tank Co, Cav Mecz Sq (20).

(For explanation of symbols, see FM 21-6.)

TABLE OF CONTENTS

		Paragraph	Page
Section	I. General	1–2	1
	II. Crew Composition and Formation	3–4	4
	III. Crew Control	5–6	6
	IV. Crew Drill	7–12	10
	V. Service of the Piece	13–18	19
	VI. Mounted Action	19–23	31
	VII. Dismounted Action	24–29	37
	VIII. Evacuation of Casualties from Tanks	30–33	46
	IX. Inspections and Maintenance	34–40	51
	X. Sight Adjustment	41–42	68
	XI. Destruction of Materiel and Equipment	43–50	71

RESTRICTED

FM 17-68

WAR DEPARTMENT FIELD MANUAL

CREW DRILL
LIGHT TANK M5 SERIES*

This manual supersedes FM 17-68, 8 June 1943.

Section I

GENERAL

1. **PURPOSE AND SCOPE.** This manual is designed to present instructional material for the platoon leader and tank commander in training members of the crew of the light tanks M5 and M5A1 for combat. It is to be used as a guide to achieve orderly, disciplined, efficient execution of mounted and dismounted action, and precision, accuracy, and speed in service of the piece. It provides a logical and thorough routine for all inspections of the vehicle and its equipment.

2. **REFERENCES.** See appendix.

---

* "For definition of military terms not defined in this manual see TM 20-205".

Figure 1. Light tank M5A1, front and rear views.

Figure 2. Light tank M5A1.

Section II

COMPOSITION AND FORMATIONS

3. COMPOSITION. The light tank crew is composed of four members:

Tank commander (loader or assistant gunner and tends voice radio)	LIEUTENANT or SERGEANT
Gunner	GUNNER
Bow Gunner (assistant driver, and radio operator in tanks equipped with SCR-506)	BOG
Driver	DRIVER

Figure 3. Dismounted posts, light tank crew.

4. FORMATIONS. a. **Dismounted posts.** The crew forms at attention in one rank. (See figure 3). The tank commander takes his post 2 yards in front of the right track, facing the front. The bow gunner, gunner and driver in order, take positions at the left of the tank commander at close interval.

b. **Mounted posts.** The crew forms mounted as follows:

(1) *Tank commander.* In the turret, standing on the floor, sitting or standing on the seat.

(2) *Bow gunner.* In the bow gunner's seat.

(3) *Gunner.* In the turret, seated at the left of the 37-mm gun with his left hand on the power traverse control handle, his right hand on the elevating handwheel, and his head against the headrest of the periscope.

(4) *Driver.* In the driver's seat.

Section III

CREW CONTROL

5. OPERATION OF INTERPHONE AND RADIO. The crew must practice continually with the interphone to attain its maximum value during combat. It is available for use at any time during the operation of the tank, but its use interrupts radio communication. Due to the differences in location of the radio and interphone facilities of the light tank M5 and M5A1, slightly different procedures are necessary in crew control. For tank signals see FM 17-5.

a. M5 light tank. As standing operating procedure, after mounting, the radio is turned on by either the driver or gunner without command, and the headsets and microphones are tested. See Preliminary Inspection for Radio Sets SCR-508, SCR-528, and SCR-538.

(1) Each crew member (except the gunner who has no interphone connection) inserts the plugs of the short cords extending from his headset into the break-away plug of the headset extension cord of his interphone control box. The microphone (of either type, throat or lip) is adjusted in place to produce maximum clarity, and connected to the break-away plug on the microphone cord of the control box.

(2) The tank commander turns his **RADIO INTERPHONE** switch to **INTERPHONE**, depresses the switch on his microphone cord, and orders: CHECK INTERPHONE. NOTE: This command is used when the crew mounts by any other method than the formalized drills given in paragraphs 8 and 25. In those drills the "Ready" report constitutes the interphone check.

(3) The bow gunner and driver, in turn, depress their microphone switches and report: BOG CHECK, DRIVER CHECK. During this procedure, each adjusts

the volume control on his interphone control box to the desired level. *Care is taken that the microphone switch does not remain in locked position thus burning out the dynamotor.* In stowing, check to see that the suspension strap is not wrapped around the hand switch, pressing down the switch button.

(4) Interphone control box positions are located as follows:

(a) *Driver.* On wall of hull to his left.

(b) *Bow gunner.* On wall of hull to his right.

(c) *Tank commander.* On rear of turret roof between the hatches. He controls his transmission by manipulating the switch on the control box marked RADIO-INTERPHONE to the type of transmission desired.

(5) The RADIO-INTERPHONE switches on the transmitter and on all control boxes, except the tank commander's control *box, are set on RADIO. This is the normal position for interphone operation.* The tank commander's switch is set on RADIO most of the time, he will change it to INTERPHONE only as he desires to communicate with his crew. Except in an emergency, *no one but the tank commander* may operate the interphone switch on his control box. In an emergency, a member of the tank crew may break in while the tank commander is on RADIO by turning his control box switch to INTERPHONE. When the tank commander is on RADIO, turning any RADIO-INTERPHONE switch to INTERPHONE will interrupt the commander's radio communication and establish interphone communication.

(6) It is the duty of each man to check his personal interphone equipment upon mounting the tank, see that it is properly maintained, and report any difficulties to the tank commander. Definite tank control commands and terminology are set forth in the following paragraph. The desirability and necessity of adhering to this specific language cannot be overemphasized. General conversation on interphones causes misunderstanding and disorder and is harmful to discipline.

b. M5A1 light tank. In this and later models, the radio is located in the turret bulge, immediately accessible to the tank commander. The gunner's interphone control box is on the roof of the turret in front of him. The tank commander's control box is on the right side of the turret. On mounting the M5A1 tank, the crew follows the same procedure as that prescribed for the M5 model with the following exceptions: the tank commander turns on the receiver, transmitter or amplifier, and sets the channel number button. Upon the command CHECK INTERPHONE, the gunner reports first, followed in order by the bow gunner and driver.

NOTE: In tanks equipped with SCR-506, two members of the crew (Bog and gunner) are qualified radio operators. The principal duty of the Bog is to operate this set, and interphone procedure is modified as required to enable him to perform his duties.

6. INTERPHONE LANGUAGE. a. Terms.

Tank Commander ____LIEUTENANT or SERGEANT
Driver _____DRIVER
Gunner _____GUNNER
Bow Gunner _____BOG
Any tank _____TANK
Armored car _____ARMORED CAR
Any unarmored vehicle_TRUCK
Infantry _____DOUGHS
Machine gun _____MACHINE GUN
Airplane _____PLANE

b. Commands for movement of tank.
To move the tank
  forward _____DRIVER MOVE OUT
To halt the tank _____DRIVER STOP
To reverse the tank ___DRIVER REVERSE
To decrease speed ____DRIVER SLOW DOWN
To turn right 90° _____DRIVER CLOCK 3 ---
                       STEADY-Y-Y-Y . . . ON
To turn left 60° _____DRIVER CLOCK 10---
                       STEADY-Y-Y-Y . . . ON

To turn right (left)
   180° ---------------DRIVER CLOCK 6 RIGHT
                        (LEFT)---STEADY-Y-Y-Y
                        . . . ON
To have driver move to-
ward a terrain feature
or reference point. The
tank being headed in
proper direction ------DRIVER MARCH ON WHITE
                        HOUSE (HILL, DEAD TREE,
                        ETC.)
To follow in column --DRIVER FOLLOW THAT
                        TANK (DRIVER FOLLOW
                        TANK NO B-9)
To follow on road or
   trail ---------------DRIVER RIGHT ON ROAD
                        (DRIVER RIGHT ON TRAIL)
To start engines -----DRIVER CRANK UP
To stop the engine ---DRIVER CUT ENGINE
To proceed at same
   speed --------------DRIVER STEADY

c. Comands for control of turret.

To traverse the turret --GUNNER TRAVERSE LEFT
                        (RIGHT)
To stop turret traverse _GUNNER STEADY-Y-Y-Y
                        . . . ON

d. Fire orders. See FM 17-12.

Section IV

CREW DRILL

7. **DISMOUNTED DRILL. a. To form light tank crew.** Being dismounted, the crew takes dismounted posts (figure 3) at the command FALL IN.

b. To break ranks. At the command FALL OUT, the crew breaks ranks. Crew members habitually fall out to the right of the tank.

c. To call off. At the command CALL OFF, the members of the crew call off in turn as follows:
  (1) Tank Commander _____ "SERGEANT" (or "LIEUTENANT")
  (2) Bow Gunner _____ "BOG"
  (3) Gunner _____ "GUNNER"
  (4) Driver _____ "DRIVER"

d. To change designations and duties. (1) At the command FALL OUT SERGEANT (BOG) (GUNNER) –

(a) The man designated to fall out moves by the rear to the left flank position and becomes driver.

(b) The crew members on the left of the vacated post move smartly to the right one position, ready to call off their new designations.

(c) The acting tank commander starts calling off as soon as the crew is re-formed in line.

(2) The movement is executed by having any member of the crew fall out except the driver.

(3) All movements are executed with snap and precision and at double time.

8. TO MOUNT LIGHT TANK CREW. Crew being at dismounted posts (figure 4).

Tank Commander	Gunner	Bow Gunner	Driver
Command PREPARE to MOUNT.			
About face.	About face.	About face.	About face.
Command MOUNT.			
Mount to right fender.	Mount to left fender.	Stand fast.	Stand fast.
			Mount to left fender.
Mount to right sponson.	Mount to left sponson.	Mount to right fender.	Enter Driver's hatch and take mounted post.
Enter turret and take mounted post.	Enter turret and take mounted post.	Enter Bog's hatch and take mounted post.	Turn on master switch.
	Turn on radio.		
Connect breakaway plugs.	Connect breakaway plugs.	Connect breakaway plugs.	Connect breakaway plugs.
Command REPORT.			
	Report "Gunner Ready".		
		Report "Bog Ready".	
			Report "Driver Ready".

Figure 4. Mounting through hatches, light tank M5A1.

9. TO CLOSE AND OPEN HATCHES. a. Crew being at mounted posts. TO CLOSE HATCHES.

Tank Commander	Gunner	Bow Gunner	Driver
Check that turret is in straight ahead position; order Gunner to traverse as necessary. Command CLOSE HATCHES. Close hatch. Raise periscopes. Command REPORT.	Traverse turret as ordered by Tank Commander. Close hatch. Raise periscope. Report "Gunner Ready".	Close hatch. Raise periscope. Report "Bog Ready".	Close hatch. Raise periscope. Report "Driver Ready".

b. Crew being mounted and hatches closed, TO OPEN HATCHES —

Tank Commander	Gunner	Bow Gunner	Driver
Check that turret is in straight ahead position; order Gunner to traverse as necessary.	Traverse gun as ordered by Tank Commander.		

Tank Commander	Gunner	Bow Gunner	Driver
Command OPEN HATCHES. Lower periscopes. Open hatch. Command REPORT.	Open hatch. Report "Gunner Ready".	Lower periscope. Open hatch. Report "Bog Ready".	Lower periscope. Open hatch. Report "Driver Ready".

10. TO DISMOUNT TANK CREW.
Hatches being open, to dismount without vehicular weapons—

Tank Commander	Gunner	Bow Gunner	Driver
Command PREPARE TO DISMOUNT	Turn off radio.		Turn off master switch.
Disconnect breakaway plugs. Command DISMOUNT.	Disconnect breakaway plugs.	Disconnect breakaway plugs.	Disconnect breakaway plugs.

Tank Commander	Gunner	Bow Gunner	Driver
Dismount to right sponson. Dismount to right fender. Take dismounted post.	Dismount to left sponson. Dismount to left fender. Take dismounted post.	Dismount to right fender. Take dismounted post.	Dismount to left fender. Take dismounted post.

11. TO DISMOUNT THROUGH ESCAPE HATCH. (Applicable only to M5A1 and later models equipped with escape hatch.) Crew being at mounted posts, to dismount without vehicular weapons.

Tank Commander	Gunner	Bow Gunner	Driver
Command THROUGH ESCAPE HATCH, PREPARE TO DISMOUNT.	Turn off radio.		Turn off master switch.
Disconnect breakaway plugs.	Disconnect breakaway plugs. Raise recoil guard. Elevate breech of gun.	Disconnect breakaway plugs. Unclamp spare parts box from escape hatch door and open the door.	Disconnect breakaway plugs.

Tank Commander	Gunner	Bow Gunner	Driver
Command DISMOUNT. Enter Bog's compartment, feet first. Dismount through escape hatch.	Move to right side of turret.	Dismount through escape hatch.	
	Enter Bog's compartment feet first. Dismount through escape hatch.	Crawl from under tank; take dismounted post.	
			Enter Bog's compartment. Dismount through escape hatch. Crawl from under tank; take dismounted post.
Crawl from under tank; take dismounted post.	Crawl from under tank; take dismounted post.		

NOTE: In some models of the light tank the Driver cannot cross the transmission into the Bog's compartment. In such cases he dismounts by passing through the turret compartment. (The Gunner must move an ammunition box from the turret opening before this can be done.)

12. PEP DRILL. To maintain the interest of crew members, frequent and unexpected periods of pep drill are interspersed in the crew drill and simulated firing routines. Pep drill is a series of precision movements executed at high speed and terminating at the position of attention, either mounted or dismounted. For example, the crews being dismounted, the platoon commander may suddenly command, IN FRONT OF YOUR TANKS, FALL IN; MOUNT: DISMOUNT; ON THE LEFT OF YOUR TANKS, FALL IN; FORWARD, MARCH; BY THE LEFT FLANK, MARCH; TO THE REAR, MARCH; MOUNT! (figure 5). Preparatory commands for mounting and dismounting are eliminated in this drill. The posts of all crew members are changed frequently. Pep drill freshens the interest of the crews, trains them to be agile in and around the tank, and increases their coordination and physical development.

(a) DISMOUNT; on the left of your tanks, FALL IN.

(b) MOUNT.

Figure 5. Pep drill.

Section V

SERVICE OF THE PIECE

13. GUN CREW. a. The gun crew, 37-mm tank gun, consists of the gunner who aims and fires the piece and the assistant gunner (tank commander) who loads the piece when not observing, and controls and adjusts fire.

b. Training in service of the piece must stress rapidity and precision of movement and teamwork.

14. POSITIONS OF GUN CREW. Positions of the gun crew are as prescribed in paragraph 4b.

15. OPERATION OF GUN. a. To open the breech. Grasp the T-handle of the crank under the breechblock and pull down until the breechblock is locked in the open position.

b. To close the breech. The insertion of a round in the gun trips the extractors and causes the breechblock to close automatically. For this reason use care in closing the breech manually as follows:

(1) Insert an empty cartridge case in the breech, base foremost, and trip the extractors. The breechblock will close, pushing the cartridge case upward.

(2) If an empty cartridge case is not available a block of wood of the proper size may be used.

(3) If necessary, the extractors may be tripped by using the fingers. This is done by pulling down on the T-handle and overcoming the tension of the closing spring. Then push the extractor lips forward with the fingers of the free hand and allow the breechblock to rise slowly. *Utmost caution must be exercised if this method is used.*

Figure 6. Turret and gun controls on combination gun mount M44, in light tank M5A1.

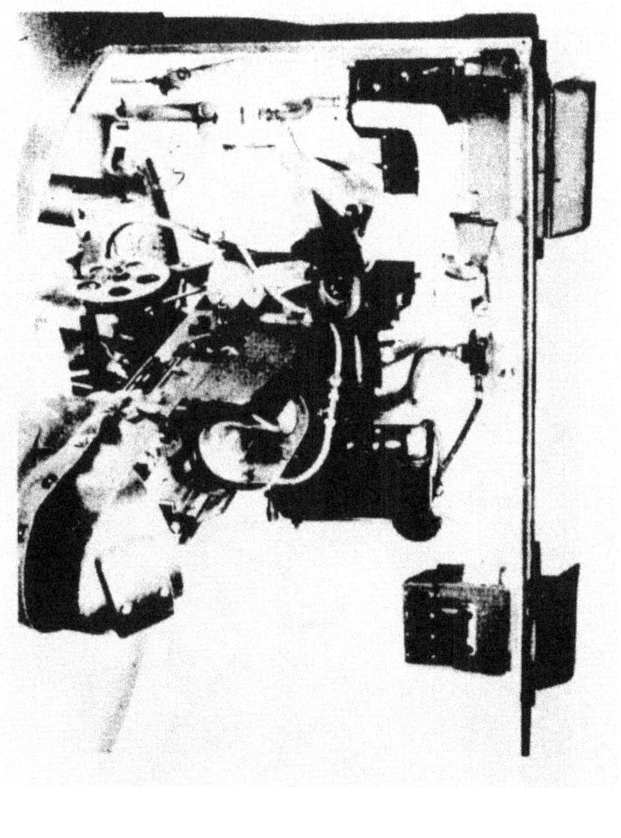

Figure 7. Left rear view of turret trainer for light tank gun crews.

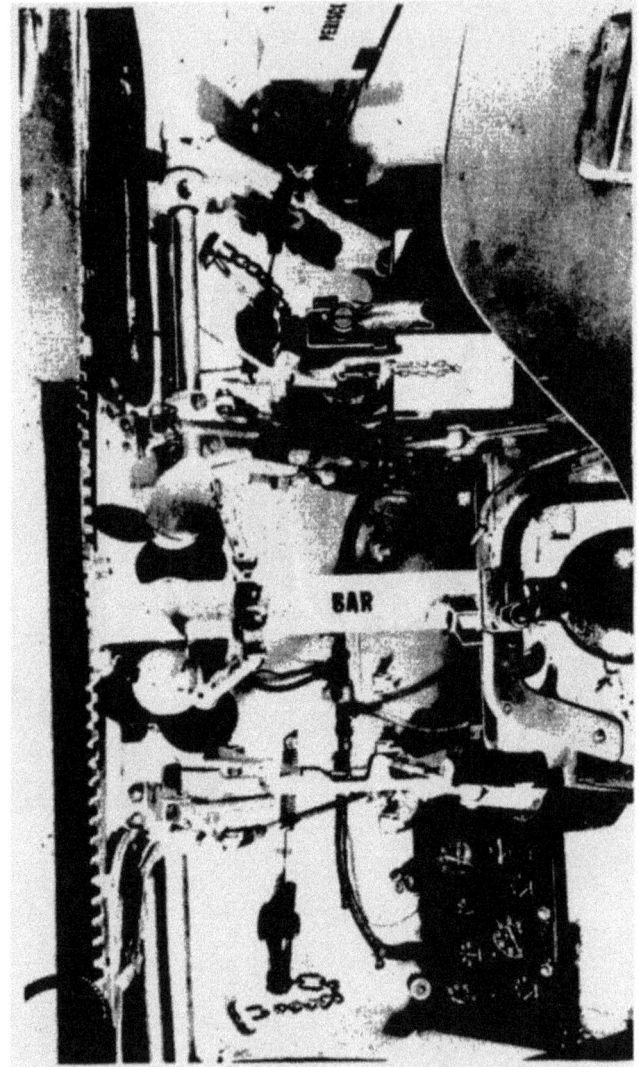

Figure 8. Driver's compartment, light tank M5.

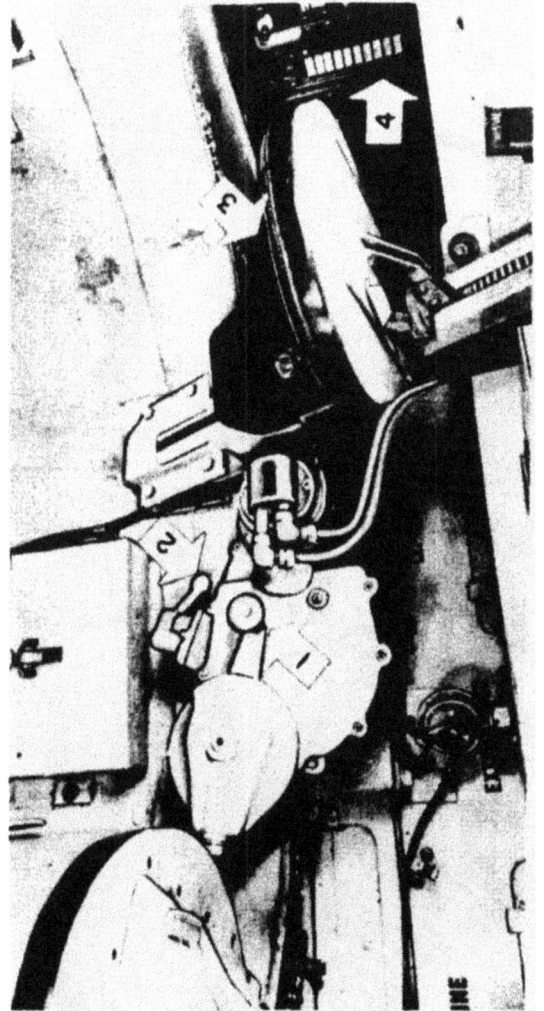

Figure 9. Turret basket, left side, light tank M5.

1. Traverse hand crank
2. Power traverse clutch lever
3. Gunner's seat
4. Radio

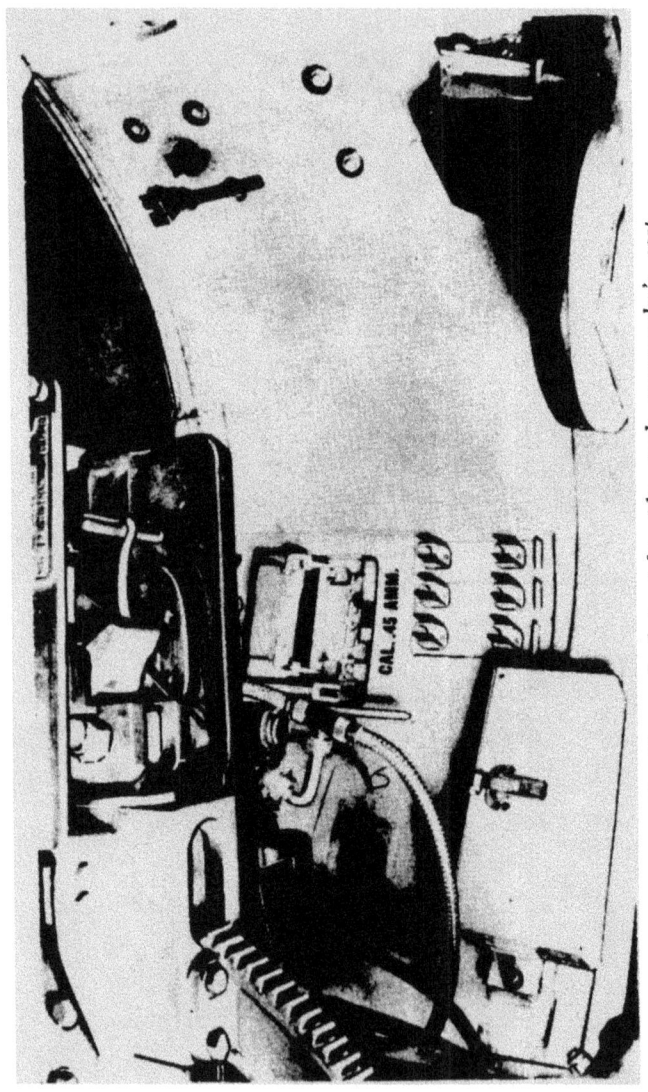

Figure 10. Turret basket, right side, tank commander's seat, light tank M5.

c. To load. (1) Open breech by pulling down on T-handle until breechblock is locked in the open position.

(2) Grasp projectile at the base with left hand, turn nose of projectile to the front, swing arm toward the breech and insert round into recess of breech ring. After nose of projectile is aligned in chamber, shove round forward sharply with the thumb on the base, following through with the arm moving upward to clear the closing breechlock. Keep arm above gun to avoid the path of recoil, and tap gunner on the back.

d. To lay the gun. Locate target through the periscope. Turn the power traverse (pistol grip) control handle, or traverse with hand crank (figure 11) in the proper direction until the vertical line of range dots (or dashes) is on the target, or the proper lead is taken. Make the final traversing motion against the greatest resistance, such as might be caused by cant in the tank. Then elevate gun until the proper range marking is on the target (see FM 17-12).

e. To fire the gun. Squeeze the safety trigger on the power traverse control handle and press the 37-mm gun switch simultaneously (figures 5 and 6). If the round fails to fire, proceed as in paragraphs 17 and 18. The gun can be fired manually with the firing button in the hub of the elevating handwheel.

f. To unload an unfired round. To unload an unfired round, pull down the T-handle and the round will be ejected into the spent case bag. The round is then returned to the rack.

g. To unload a stuck round. Whenever possible, rounds are removed from guns by shooting them out. When an unfired round is stuck in the gun and cannot be dislodged from the breech by using the rim of an empty cartridge case to pry it out, the gunner, under direct supervision of an officer, or the tank commander, if no officer is present, inserts the rammer in the muzzle of the gun, pushes it through the bore until it meets the round, and then shoves the round out of the gun. DO

1. Periscope headrest
2. Recoil adjuster knob
3. Stiffness adjuster knob
4. Firing switches for 37-mm gun and co-axial machine gun
5. Power traverse (pistol grip) control handle
6. Safety trigger
7. Elevating handwheel
8. T-handle
9. Machine gun solenoid
10. Gyro control unit.
11. Periscopic sight M4, w/telescope M40
12. Worm and sector gear
13. Oil reservoir (filler gauge)

Figure 11. Gunner's controls, combination gun mount M23.

NOT STRIKE THE ROUND WITH THE RAMMER. If pressure will not dislodge a round, tap the end of the rammer staff lightly with a block of wood, alternating tapping and pressure.

h. For further malfunctions and their remedies see paragraph 17.

16. SAFETY PRECAUTIONS. a. Before firing, and during lulls in firing, inspect the gun to see that there are no obstructions in the bore.

b. In loading the gun, take care not to dent or burr the projectile by striking it against the breech ring. *Clean ammunition before loading*. Never attempt to disassemble a round.

c. The gunner fires the gun only when the loader (tank commander) has tapped him on the back to signal that the gun is loaded and ready.

d. The 37-mm gun is fired only when the tank engine(s) are running or when at least one of the turret hatches is open to carry off the powder fumes.

e. Any individual who observes a condition which makes firing dangerous will immediately call or signal "CEASE FIRING".

f. Firing will cease immediately at the command or signal "CEASE FIRING", regardless of the source of the command.

g. Before loading, the solenoid firing devices are checked to insure that they are not stuck.

h. Tank weapons, except AA gun, are fired only when the Driver's and Bog's hatches are closed.

17. MALFUNCTIONS AND REMEDIES. Malfunctions of the gun are divided into three general classes: failure to fire, failure to load, and failure to extract. The most likely malfunctions are failures to fire. Malfunctions which are not the result of broken or worn parts are generally due to carelessness and improper cleaning of the parts and ammunition.

a. Failure of gun to fire.

Cause	Remedy
1. Safety lever on "Safe".	1. Put lever on "Fire".
2. Gun out of battery.	2. Push gun into battery; paragraph 18.
3. Defective firing mechanism.	3. Repair or replace.
4. Defective ammunition.	4. Use a new round.
5. Broken or defective firing pin.	5. Replace.
6. Broken cocking lever.	6. Replace.
7. Broken cocking fork.	7. Replace.
8. Broken cocking lugs on the percussion mechanism.	8. Replace.
9. Weak firing spring.	9. Replace.

b. Failure of gun to load.

Cause	Remedy
1. Dirty round.	1. Remove round and clean.
2. Dirty chamber.	2. Remove round and clean chamber.
3. Bulged round.	3. Use a new round.
4. Dirty breechblock recess.	4. Clean.
5. Worn or broken extractor lips.	5. Replace.
6. Bent or undersize rim of round.	6. Use a new round.
7. Defective closing mechanism.	7. Repair or replace.
8. Burrs on bearing surfaces of breechblock and breech ring.	8. Report to Ordnance.
9. Gun out of battery.	9. Put gun in battery, see paragraph 18.
10. Weak closing spring.	10. Replace.

c. Failure of gun to extract.

Cause	Remedy
1. Broken extractor lips.	1. Pry or ram out empty case and replace extractors.
2. Undersize or bent rim of round.	2. Pry or ram out.
3. Broken operating crank.	3. Pry or ram out empty case. Replace crank.
4. Broken operating lug.	4. Pry or ram out empty round. Replace operating crank.

18. **IMMEDIATE ACTION.** The sequence following (trouble shooting) is done immediately after the gun fails to fire during combat, and repair or replacement of parts cannot be effected immediately, as can be done in garrison.

a. **Gun out of battery.** (1) Push gun into battery by hand, relay, and fire.

(2) If gun still fails to fire, recock by hand (use board if necessary) and attempt to fire two times. If it does not fire, remove round to determine the cause of misfire. (See AR 750-10)

(3) If gun will not go into battery by hand, fully depress muzzle. Slowly unscrew rear recoil drain plug, being careful not to remove it entirely. An excessive amount of oil might escape if the gun suddenly started back into battery. Allow oil to drain from around the plug until it will no longer flow from cylinder, then tighten filler plug and push gun back into battery by hand.

(4) If gun will not go into battery after checking recoil cylinder, check for dirt, burrs, and lack of lubrication between the bearing surfaces of the recoil cylinder slides (rails) and sleigh guides. Clean, remove burrs, lubricate, reload, relay, and fire. (For a thorough cleaning and inspection of these parts, unscrew

coupler key nut and remove coupler key; then pull barrel assembly to rear.) NOTE: It may be possible to continue gun in action by pushing it into battery each time. However, at the first opportunity the gun should be checked and repaired.

b. Gun in battery. (1) *Breechblock not closed.*

(*a*) Close it manually, relay, and fire.

(*b*) If it will not close, see if ammunition is seated. If ammunition will not seat, remove round, reload, relay and fire. If ammunition still will not seat, clean chamber, reload, relay, and fire.

c. Ammunition is seated. Check for broken or worn extractor and closing spring, replacing if necessary. Clean and lubricate bearing surfaces of breechblock if necessary.

(1) *Breechblock is closed.*

(*a*) Recock piece. If cocking action shows that piece is still cocked (indicated by no resistance other than the cocking lever plunger spring), examine for bent or broken trigger arm, and for malfunction of trigger actuator mechanism. Replace parts if possible, relay and fire. If trigger mechanism is not defective, remove firing spring retainer and check for weak or broken firing spring.

(*b*) If cocking action indicates that the sear lug has been released from the sear shoulder (indicated by heavy resistance to cocking action), relay and fire. If gun still fails to fire after twice repeating this action, remove percussion mechanism; clean, lubricate, replace defective parts, recock, relay, and fire.

(*c*) If gun fails to fire, unload, load with a new round, relay and fire.

(*d*) If cocking action shows that the sear lug will not remain engaged on the sear shoulder, disassemble breechblock, clean and replace defective parts.

Section VI

MOUNTED ACTION

19. PREPARE TO FIRE. The crew being at mounted posts, with hatches open.

Tank Commander	Gunner	Bow Gunner	Driver
Command PREPARE TO FIRE.			
Inspect bore and chamber of 37-mm.	Check solenoids and manual firing controls.	Close hatch; raise and clean periscope.	Close hatch; raise and clean periscope.
Half-load coaxial machine gun.	Help load coaxial machine gun.		
Unlock turret traverse lock.	Unlock gun traveling lock and turret friction clamp.	Report "Bog's hatch closed".	Report "Driver's hatch closed".
Clean exterior of Gunner's and Tank Commander's sights.	Wipe off sights. Make field check of sights (see Par 41).	Unlock bow gun traveling lock.	Start auxiliary generator.

Tank Commander	Gunner	Bow Gunner	Driver
	Check manual traverse; engage power traverse. Turn stabilizer on if situation warrants. Close hatch.	Half-load bow gun.	
Command REPORT.	Report "Gunner Ready".	Report "Bog Ready".	Report "Driver Ready".

20. DUTIES IN FIRING. Tank prepared to fire with guns loaded.

Tank Commander	Gunner	Bow Gunner	Driver
Give fire order as prescribed in FM 17-12. Reload 37-mm gun (except when observing from open turret hatch). Inspect all rounds	Fire on targets as ordered by Tank Commander. Reload 37-mm gun if	Fire on designated targets and on emergency targets that appear. When not firing, observe	After fire order is issued, avoid changing course and maintain constant speed if moving. (Steer only to

before loading, and wipe off if necessary.

Tank Commander is observing from open hatch, or if he is in position where he cannot load.

in assigned sector.

avoid obstacles, or if change of direction is ordered; avoid excess steering or small changes). Warn Gunner if about to pass over rough ground or if about to change course by calling ROUGH, or CHANGING COURSE.

Signal ready by tapping Gunner on back.

If necessary, change recoil knob setting. Call MISFIRE if 37-mm fails to fire. Recock gun and fire. If gun fails to fire after twice repeating this action, see Par. 17.

When gunner calls MISFIRE, check that breech is closed and gun is in battery. Help Gunner recock gun.

Select speed which can be maintained over the particular terrain.

When tank fires from stationary position, continue to run engines unless ordered otherwise.

Tank Commander	Gunner	Bow Gunner	Driver
When Gunner calls STOPPAGE, reduce stoppage in coaxial machine gun. Fire coaxial machine gun at Gunner's command if solenoid fails to operate. Fire antiaircraft machine gun. Control Driver over interphone.	Call STOPPAGE if coaxial machine gun fails to fire. Notify Tank Commander when to fire coaxial machine gun in case solenoid fails to operate. During lulls in firing, observe in assigned sector.		

21. TO SECURE GUNS.

Tank Commander	Gunner	Bow Gunner	Driver
Command CEASE FIRING, SECURE GUNS. Clear coaxial MG, unload 37-mm gun, inspect bore and close breech. Lower periscopes, open hatch.	Traverse turret to front. Turn off firing switch. Turn off power traverse, engage	Clear Bow MG. Lock bow gun traveling lock. Lower periscope, open hatch.	Turn off auxiliary generator. Lower periscope, open hatch. Raise seat to convoy position.

	manual traverse.	Dispose of empty cartridge cases.	
	Turn off stabilizer; engage manual elevating gear.		
	Open hatch.		
Refill 37-mm ready racks.	Help refill 37-mm ready racks.		
Dispose of empty cartridge cases.	Help dispose of empty cartridge cases.		
Lock turret traversing lock.	Lock friction clamp.		
	Lock gun traveling lock.		
			Put on tape muzzle covers.
If situation permits, order Bog to swab bore.	Make field check of sights.	If so ordered, dismount, swab bore, and remount. Put on bow machine gun tape muzzle cover.	
Command REPORT.	Report "Gunner Ready".	Report "Bog Ready".	Report "Driver Ready"

22. TO LOAD AMMUNITION. Wipe off, load and stow 37-mm gun ammunition with great care to avoid burring the rotating band, or denting the case. (See TM 9-1900). Different lots should be segregated. During periods between firing, ammunition is restowed to the most accessible racks. Test each round of ammunition by loading in gun.

23. TO LOAD ALL WEAPONS. a. The tank gun is loaded on order; this is normally the fire order, but some types of action will dictate loading prior to the appearance of the target. Machine guns are clear until the command PREPARE TO FIRE, when they are half-loaded. When the fire order is given, however, or the unit is deployed for combat, all machine guns are fully loaded. This does not necessarily apply to the AA gun, which is elevated and half-loaded as the tactical situation demands.

b. When the tank commander is not in a position to load (observing from the top of the turret), he commands LOAD SHOT (HE). At the command the gunner loads as directed.

Section VII

DISMOUNTED ACTION

24. TO FIGHT ON FOOT THROUGH HATCHES. a. Crew being at mounted posts, hatches open.

NOTE: In all drills which include manning of submachine gun, it is assumed that the tank is equipped with four submachine guns M3. Therefore, when the cal .30 MG is not dismounted to fight on foot, all crew members will dismount with submachine gun M3, plus a submachine ammunition case containing six 30-round clips.

Tank Commander	Gunner	Bow Gunner	Driver
Command PREPARE TO FIGHT ON FOOT.			
Order distribution of grenades.	Procure grenades as ordered.	Procure grenades as ordered.	
Disconnect break-away plugs.	Disconnect break-away plugs.	Disconnect break-away plugs.	
Secure submachine gun and ammunition carrying case.			Clear bow gun (if loaded).

37

Tank Commander	Gunner	Bow Gunner	Driver
Command DISMOUNT.			
Dismount with submachine gun ammunition and binoculars.	Dismount to receive spare parts roll and spare bolt assembly from driver.		Pass spare parts roll and spare bolt assembly to Gunner.
	Receive three boxes cal .30 ammunition; place in front of tank.	Pass three boxes cal .30 ammunition to Gunner.	
Dismount tripod*, lay in front of tank. Pick up two boxes cal .30 ammunition. Lead crew to MG position.	Receive bow MG from Bog.	Dismount bow gun and pass it to Gunner. Dismount from tank, pick up tripod and one box cal .30 ammunition.	Remain in tank; drive it to concealment. Disconnect breakaway plugs. Move to turret; connect breakaway plugs to Tank Commander's control box. Maintain contact with Platoon Leader.

Tank Commander	Gunner	Bow Gunner	Driver
Supervise firing of MG; cover gun crew with submachine gun.	Mount gun.*	Mount tripod.	Man AA or 37-mm gun from turret, as situation demands.
	Man gun as #2.	Man gun as #1.	

*Make sure pintle and elevating mechanism are in tripod case. If not, Bog obtains them from spare parts box and passes to Gunner.

b. The dismounted crew moves to the position indicated by the tank commander, or in drill as indicated in figures 12 and 13. The crew members take posts and perform duties of the crew of a ground mounted machine gun as prescribed for gun drill in FM 23-55.

c. In combat it is assumed that the tank will be moved to a concealed position if possible, before the crew dismounts. The driver remains in the tank, moves it to concealment, and mans the antiaircraft machine gun or tank cannon as the situation demands.

25. TO REMOUNT FROM ACTION THROUGH HATCHES.

Tank Commander	Gunner	Bow Gunner	Driver
Command OUT OF ACTION, MOUNT.			
Supervise taking MG out of action.	Dismount gun.	Fold tripod, lay tripod and cal .30 ammunition box in front of tank.	

Tank Commander	Gunner	Bow Gunner	Driver
	Pass bow MG to Bog.	Take mounted post. Receive bow MG and mount it.	
Strap tripod on tank fender.	Pass spare parts roll and bolt assembly to Driver.		Resume mounted post.
Mount to turret, taking submachine gun and ammunition.	Pass 3 boxes cal. .30 ammunition to Bog.	Receive and stow 3 boxes cal. .30 ammunition from Gunner.	Receive and stow spare parts roll and bolt assembly.
Connect breakaway plugs.	Connect breakaway plugs.	Connect breakaway plugs.	Connect breakaway plugs.
Command REPORT.	Report "Gunner Ready".	Report "Bog Ready".	Report "Driver Ready".

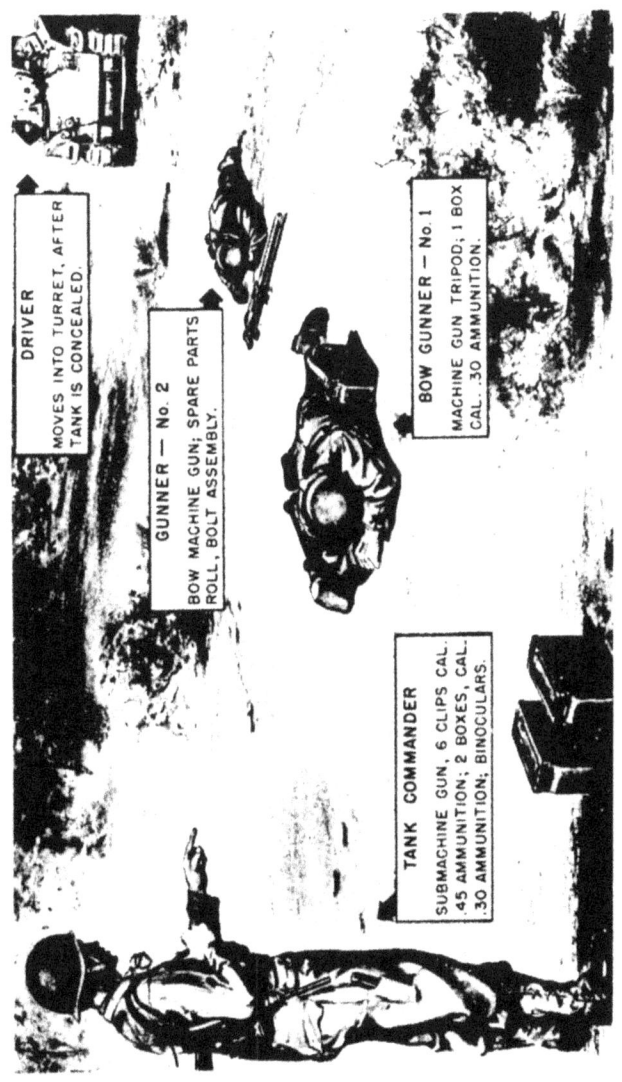

Figure 12. Dismounted action, crew formed for drill (tank commander instructing).

Figure 13. Posts of dismounted crew in action.

26. ACTION IN CASE OF FIRE. a. Fire in engine compartment. The first crew member to discover the fire calls ENGINE FIRE—

Tank Commander	Gunner	Bow Gunner	Driver
Disconnect breakaway plugs		Disconnect breakaway plugs	
Receive "speed" wrench from Bog.	Pull fixed fire extinguisher control handle.	Pass "speed" wrench (from tool box) to Tank Commander.	Stop engines.
Dismount to rear of tank; open engine doors with wrench.	Receive hand extinguisher from Bog. Relay hand extinguisher to Tank Commander.	Pass hand extinguisher to Gunner in turret.	
Receive extinguisher from Gunner, stand by to use it in case fixed extinguisher does not put out fire.	Remain at post for further orders.	Dismount; go to rear of tank and assist Tank Commander.	Remain at post for further orders.

b. Fire in turret or driver compartment. The first crew member to discover the fire calls TURRET (HULL) FIRE. The tank is stopped and engines shut off. Fire extinguishers are passed to men nearest fire and other crew members help them in any way possible to extinguish the flame. The turret is traversed in any direction which will aid crew to reach fire with extinguishers.

27. TO ABANDON TANK. If it becomes necessary to abandon tank, the crew proceeds as in paragraph 10, 24, or 26, with the following changes or additions:

a. Time permitting deliberate action, the tank commander displays the flag signal DISREGARD MY MOVEMENTS, and supervises the disabling of those weapons which remain in the tank. Backplates are removed from machine guns and the percussion mechanism from the tank gun. All similar spare parts are also removed. Individual weapons and maximum possible ammunition loads are carried. The driver dismounts in order with the rest of the crew.

b. Ordinarily the tank is abandoned as a result of a direct hit which either causes it to catch fire or disables it so that it becomes a vulnerable target. There may be a time interval of as little as five seconds in which the crew can escape without further injury. At the command ABANDON TANK, crew members throw open hatches, climb out, jump to the ground and take cover at a safe distance from the tank. It is particularly important in case of fire to hold the breath until clear of the vehicle. Inhaling the fumes and smoke of the fire may injure the lungs and will at least incapacitate the individual for a time.

28. ADVICE TO INSTRUCTORS. a. Disciplined and effective dismounted action requires long and arduous drill. Satisfactory results are obtained only by painstaking repetition of each movement.

b. Training in dismounted action is undertaken in the field rather than in the tank park. Crews are required to dismount to fight on foot on all types of terrain and under every variety of simulated combat conditions with full loads of ammunition. Rough terrain complicates the problem of dismounting from the escape hatch and develops ingenuity and physical agility not possible in tank park training.

c. Instructors explain and demonstrate to tank crews how necessary to their safety and success in combat is a high state of training in dismounted action. They must point out that dismounted action from disabled tank taken under small arms fire usually is practicable only from the escape hatch, and that skill and practice in use of the escape hatch will pay dividends. The escape door is kept clean and well lubricated so that its release is immediate and positive. Frequent inspection of the mechanism is made by the tank commander to see that the locking rods are not bent.

29. PARK AND BIVOUAC PRECAUTIONS. a. Always have a guide when moving a tank in park or bivouac.

b. Keep at least 10 feet in front of tank and to one side of its path when directing the tank forward or backward in park or bivouac.

c. Walk, do not run while guiding a tank.

d. Mount and dismount without using tube of gun as a hand hold, or breech end of gun as a foot hold in entering turret.

Section VIII

EVACUATION OF CASUALTIES FROM TANKS

30. GENERAL. a. The drill prescribed in the following paragraphs is for use in training crew members so that any two of them may evacuate casualties with maximum efficiency. A tank disabled by an enemy projectile may expect another hit without delay. When ammunition is ignited, evacuation must be effected in a few seconds. Therefore speed, rather than care in handling, is the primary consideration in removing a casualty from a tank.

b. Evacuation of casualties is undertaken only:

(1) When the tank is disabled.

(2) When the position of the casualty in the tank prevents the crew from functioning.

(3) At the rallying point.

After evacuation, the casualty may be carried to a protected area where emergency first-aid is administered.

31. METHODS AND DEVICES. Not more than two men can work effectively at a single hatch opening. If the man nearest the casualty is unhurt, and tactical considerations permit, he can help by remaining inside and improvising a sling (made up of pistol belts, waist belts, or field bag straps, see FM 17-80), or by moving the casualty to a position where he can be grasped from above and then aid in boosting him out. However, speed will usually dictate that the casualty be grasped by his clothing or by his arms for removal (figures 14 and 15). If there are injuries which will be aggravated by such methods, and time permits, some form of sling may be improvised to relieve that part from further injury (figure 16).

Figure 14. Evacuation of bog with arms crossed.

Figure 15. Evacuation of bog down front slope plate.

Figure 16. Evacuation of gunner with two pistol belts.

32. TO EVACUATE GUNNER (TANK COMMANDER). Crew being at mounted posts. (Note: The duties of No. 1 and No. 2 of evacuation team are interchangeable. The first man to realize the situation assumes the initiative as No. 1).

No. 1	No. 2
Command EVACUATE GUNNER (TANK COMMANDER)	
Mount to top of turret.	Throw first-aid kit (kept in accessible spot in turret) to ground.
	Mount to top of turret.
Slip pistol belt under each arm of gunner.	Pass pistol belt to No. 1.
Lift casualty through hatch.	Lift casualty through hatch.

No. 1	No. 2
	Hold body in a sitting position on hatch cover.
Lower casualty to left sponson (or protected side, if tank is disabled).	Lower casualty to left sponson (or protected side if tank is disabled).
Jump to ground; support lower portion of body as casualty is moved off tank.	Jump to ground; support upper portion of body as casualty is moved off tank.
Carry casualty to a protected area.	Help No. 1 carry casualty to a protected area.
Report location and condition of casualty.	

33. TO EVACUATE BOG (DRIVER). Crew being at mounted posts.

No. 1	No. 2
Command: EVACUATE BOG (DRIVER).	
Descend through turret opening into Bog compartment, if necessary to open locked hatch cover.	Move to Bog hatch opening.
Throw out first-aid kit.	Straddle 37-mm gun, facing rearward.
Cross arms of casualty; pull one arm through hatch as No. 2 pulls on other arm.	Pull one arm of casualty through hatch as No. 1 pulls on other arm.
Turn body to face rearward as it is lifted out.	Turn body to face rearward as it is lifted out.
	Rest body in a supported position on rim of hatch opening.

No. 1

Jump to ground in front of tank; support trunk of body as it falls backward over forward slope of tank.

Carry casualty to a protected area.

Report location and condition of casualty.

No. 2

Allow body to fall back into No. 1's arms. Make sure legs are freed from hatch opening.

Jump to ground; support lower portion of body as it is carried to a protected area.

NOTE: In case a large man is to be evacuated, one man of team may have to enter vehicle and assist from the inside.

Section IX

INSPECTIONS AND MAINTENANCE

34. GENERAL. a. The tank commander is responsible for seeing that all inspections are made. He receives reports from the various crew members relative to their individual inspections, and he indicates in his report anything requiring the service of maintenance personnel. In supervising first echelon maintenance he uses his discretion in delegating additional responsibilities to other crew members.

b. Inspection covers all personal equipment and weapons, vehicle equipment and weapons and mechanical features of the vehicle. In combat it includes a check of the application of protective cream by the crew members. Checks of instruments, lights, siren, track, suspension system, and engine performance are made in accordance with provisions of the appropriate technical manual; the driver fills in his Driver's Report indicating required maintenance work. The Driver's Report should be carefully and thoroughly prepared. Any irregularity noted and entered on the report, which is not repaired before the tank is used again, should be re-entered on the report continually until it has been properly taken care of.

35. BEFORE OPERATION INSPECTION. Tank locked and covered with tarpaulin. (NOTE: For training purposes, the inspection is divided into four phases, each phase being completed by all crew members before the next phase is begun. Crew members use tools as needed and report and correct deficiencies as found).

PHASE A

Tank Commander	Gunner	Bow Gunner	Driver
Command FALL IN: PREPARE FOR INSPECTION.			
Inspect crew.	Stand inspection.	Stand inspection.	Stand inspection.
Command PERFORM BEFORE OPERATION INSPECTION.			
Supervise inspection.	Help remove tarpaulin.	Help remove and fold tarpaulin.	Remove and fold tarpaulin (3' x 6')
Fill out trip ticket during inspection.			
Inspect outside equipment.	Mount and unlock tank.	Check for water, fuel and oil leaks around and under tank.	Lay tarpaulin to right of tank.

Receive and assemble rammer staff from Bog and MG cleaning rod and rags from gunner.	Open turret hatches; enter turret. Check that turret guns are clear. Move to Driver's compartment; unlock Driver's and Bog's hatches. Pass MG cleaning rod and rags to Tank Commander. Pass tools out to Driver. Receive and stow gun covers; clear bow guns. Stow breech covers. Open fuel shut-off valve.	Check radiators and fuel tanks for level. Pass rammer staff to Tank Commander. Check final drives for oil level.	Remove cannon muzzle cover, and bow gun cover. Receive tools from Gunner. Pass gun covers to Gunner. Lay tools on tarpaulin and check them. (Figure 17).
Command REPORT.	Report "Gunner Ready".	Report "Bog Ready".	Report "Driver Ready".

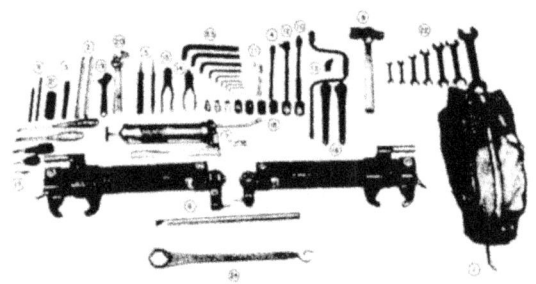

Figure 17. Vehicular tools furnished each light tank (see SNL G-103). (The number and position of tools for a formal inspection is a command decision.)

1. Bag, tool
2. Bars, utility (2)
3. Chisel, machs, hand, cold
4. Extension, socket wrench, plain, 10"
5. Files, A.S., 6" & 8" (2)
6. Fixture, track connecting and link pulling w/handle (commonly called "track jack")
7. Gun, lubr., pressure, hand
8. Hammer, machs, ball peen, 32 oz
9. Handle, cross extension, socket wrench, 8"
10. Handle, hinged socket wrench, 12", w/crossbar
11. Handle, socket wrench, offset, dble-end
12. Handle, "T", sliding, socket wrench
13. Joint, universal, socket wrench
14. Pliers, comb., slip-jt, 8"
15. Pliers, side-cutting, fl-nose, 8"
16. Ratchets, reversible, socket wrench, 9" (2)
17. Screwdrivers, including one non-magnetic for Pioneer compass (5)
18. Sockets, 1/2" sq-drive, dble-hex, 7/16" to 3/8" (9)
19. Wrench, adj., sgle-end, 8"
20. Wrench, adj., sgle-end, 12"
21. Wrench, brake, socket, w/handle
22. Wrenches, engrs, dble-hd, 5/16" to 1-3/8" (7)
23. Wrenches, socket head set screws, 1/8" hex to 3/4" hex (10)
24. Wrench, trailing idler wheel nut & track adjusting
25. Wrench, socket, speeder

PHASE B

Tank Commander	Gunner	Bow Gunner	Driver
Command PERFORM PHASE B. Assist Gunner in sight adjustment.	Make sight adjustment. See paragraph 42.	Check with Driver that master switch is off. Open engine compartment doors. Check following: Trigger type oil can. Engine oil levels. Engine compartment for water, oil and fuel leaks. Accessories and drives for adjustment and security.	Enter Driver's seat. Check that master switch is off. Inspect and check following: Battery. Oil cans and oil for vehicle. Transfer unit and differential oil level. Steering levers, parking brakes. Transmission and transfer levers for operation.
Swab bore of all guns. Put tape muzzle covers on all guns.	Open gun breech. Check following: Coaxial and AA MG and adjust headspace. 37-mm ammunition. Cal .30 ammunition. 37-mm and MG mounts (close breech).		

Tank Commander	Gunner	Bow Gunner	Driver
Command REPORT.		Air cleaners and connections. Close engine compartment doors.	Auxiliary generator oil level. Start generator; check operation.
	Report "Gunner Ready".	Report "Bog Ready".	Report "Driver Ready".

PHASE C

Tank Commander	Gunner	Bow Gunner	Driver
Command PERFORM PHASE C.		Notify Driver to start engines.	When notified by Bog, turn on master switch.
Inspect right track and suspension system. Direct Driver to move forward one tank length.	Check following: Oil in turret reservoir. Oil can and stabilizer oil.	Inspect left track and suspension system.	Start engines. Check instruments, warning lights and siren. Move tank as directed by Tank Commander.
Check right support rollers, bogie	All firing controls.	Check left support rollers, bogie	

wheels, idler and sprocket as tank moves forward.	Turn on turret master switch.	wheels, idler wheel and sprocket as tank moves forward.		
Inspect that part of track not visible before.		Inspect that part of track not visible before.		
Check for tightness of wedge nuts and sprocket ring cap screws.	Check stabilizer operation, oil reservoir connections and pump.	Check for tightness of wedge nuts and sprocket ring cap screws.		Stop engines.
				Receive and stow tools.
Replace tools in bag and pass bag to Driver.			Assist Driver in checking driving and blackout lights.	Check driving and blackout lights.
			Check MG tripod case for pintle and elevating mechanism.	
			Install radio antenna.	
			Replace tarpaulin on rear deck.	

Tank Commander	Gunner	Bow Gunner	Driver
Pass rammer staff to Bog and cleaning rod to Gunner. Mount to turret.	Receive and stow machine gun cleaning rod. Check with Driver and Bog that their hatches are closed. Check manual elevation, operation of hand and power traverse, and turret lock.	Receive and stow rammer staff. Mount and close hatch.	Close hatch.
Assist in checking recoil oil. Connect breakaway plugs. Command REPORT (interphone check)	Check recoil cylinder oil. Connect breakaway plugs. Report "Gunner Ready".	Connect breakaway plugs. Report "Bog Ready".	Connect breakaway plugs. Report "Driver Ready".

NOTE: In later models of the Light Tank M5A1, there is an *emergency ignition switch* on the right side of the hull roof. This switch is left in the "ON" position except in emergencies, when it is used by the Tank Commander or other personnel within reach.

PHASE D

Tank Commander	Gunner	Bow Gunner	Driver
Command PERFORM PHASE D. Check following: Gun books, Manuals, Accident Forms, Check Chart, Driver's permit, Periscope, spare, and spare head. Safety belt. Make first echelon check of radio and interphone system. (See Par. 41)	Check transmission oil levels. Notify Driver to start engines. Check following: Safety belt, Hull compass, Periscope, spare, spare heads, Grenades, Presence of spare parts, tools and accessories for all guns.	Check bow gun and adjust headspace; put on cartridge bag. Check following: Bow MG ammunition, Periscope, spare, and spare head. Flag set, Fire extinguishers, Decontaminating apparatus. Vehicular first-aid kit, Crew rations. Escape hatch operation, Water cans, Canvas bucket,	Open hatch. Check following: Cooking stove, Periscope, spare, and spare head. Safety belt. Start engines when notified by Gunner. Constantly observe operation of engines for smoothness, synchronization, unusual noises.

Tank Commander	Gunner	Bow Gunner	Driver
Command REPORT.		Safety belt. Open hatch	
	Report "Gunner Ready".		
		Report "Bog Ready".	
			Report "Driver Ready".
Complete trip ticket. Report READY to Platoon Leader.			

NOTE: The flame thrower, on tanks so equipped, is checked in this phase. The crew member using the weapon checks its condition, mechanism, and the fuel level in its tank in accordance with the appropriate published guide. Where it is used as an alternate weapon to the bow machine gun, it is mounted on order of the tank commander.

36. INSPECTION DURING OPERATION.
This is a continuous process of checking by all crew members.

Tank Commander	Gunner	Bow Gunner	Driver
Remain alert for unusual noises or conditions. Assist Driver to avoid	Check following: Security of turret lock. Security of gun.	Watch instruments and warning lights. Listen for unusual noises.	Check all instruments carefully. Check controls. Listen for unusual noises.

Tank Commander	Gunner	Bow Gunner	Driver
obstacles that would cause injury to tank or crew. Check radio interphone system, and security of radio antenna. Check security of AA gun, stowage, and equipment.	Stabilizer operation.	Check security of bow gun.	

37. INSPECTION AT THE HALT. The length of halt determines the extent of this inspection. Items listed below are in order of normal priority.

Tank Commander	Gunner	Bow Gunner	Driver
Command PERFORM HALT INSPECTION. Supervise halt inspection (if required to dismount the Gunner must stand by AA gun.)	Clean sights and periscopes. Make field check of sights (par 41). Check following: Security of guns and mounts.	Disconnect breakaway plugs. Dismount and close hatch. Check final drives for leaks, excessive temperatures.	Disconnect breakaway plugs. Idle engine 4-5 minutes before stopping. Check engine synchronization and unusual noises.

Tank Commander	Gunner	Bow Gunner	Driver
	Stabilizer connections. Turret mechanism. (Check that bow hatches are closed.)	Check under tank for water, oil, or fuel leaks. Check radiators for level, leaks. Check fuel tanks for level and leaks.	Check instruments, warning lights, parking brakes. Cut engines, close hatch and dismount. Open engine compartment doors. Make visual check of engine compartment for fuel, water and oil leaks, security of accessories. Check engine oil levels.
Stand by AA gun.	Radio antenna. Security of equipment in general. Place gun in traveling position. Lock turret lock. Check stowage of equipment in turret.	Check presence and security of outside equipment. Check and clean suspension system. Check presence and security of outside equipment. Help check air cleaners. Take mounted post. Clean periscope. Connect breakaway plugs.	Close engine compartment doors. Check air cleaners. Mount Driver's seat. Clean periscope. Connect breakaway plugs.

Tank Commander	Gunner	Bow Gunner	Driver
Command REPORT.			
	Report "Gunner Ready".		
		Report "Bog Ready".	
			Report "Driver Ready".
Report READY to Platoon Leader.			

38. AFTER OPERATION MAINTENANCE. a. After the operation the tank is immediately given whatever servicing and maintenance is needed to prepare it in every way for further sustained action. *This servicing covers all the points listed in the Before Operation Inspection and covers them in the same order, with obvious modifications.* (For example, the tank is locked at the end of the inspection instead of being unlocked at the beginning; the check for leaks under the tank is more effective after it has stood for a while; battery switches are turned off rather than on and only after all checks requiring use of battery power; equipment is covered and stowed rather than being uncovered and made ready for use).

b. The tank will be completely cleaned, serviced, and replenished (fuel, oil—all types, grease, coolant, ammunition—all types, first aid kit, water, and rations). *All special precautions against fire will be observed while refueling.* Crew members will perform the following additional operations not covered in the Before Operation Inspection.

Tank Commander	Gunner	Bow Gunner	Driver
Command PERFORM AFTER OPERATION MAINTENANCE.	Clean weapons.		Idle engines 4 to 5 minutes before stopping.
Forward completed trip ticket to platoon leader, and report of all necessary 2d echelon maintenance, fuel, lubricants, ammunition and rations required.		Help Driver clean tank.	Clean tank suspension and outside of tank.
		Help Gunner clean weapons.	Help Gunner clean weapons.

39. PERIODIC ADDITIONAL SERVICES. NOTE: In garrison these services are performed weekly; on maneuvers or in combat they are performed after each field operation.

Tank Commander	Gunner	Bow Gunner	Driver
Command FALL IN: PREPARE FOR INSPECTION.			
Inspect crew.	Stand inspection.	Stand inspection.	Stand inspection.

Command				
PERFORM PERIODIC INSPECTION.	Enter turret.	Tighten all wedge nuts, and inspect track and suspension system.	Enter Driver's compartment.
Inspect and supervise work of crew members.		Tighten all loose bolts, nuts and connections outside tank.	Clean battery and case thoroughly. Make hydrometer reading. Check water level. Charge if necessary.
	Tighten all loose bolts, nuts and connections in turret.		Tighten all loose bolts, nuts and connections in compartment.
	Lubricate gun and mount as needed. Check and clean parts and tools for weapons.	Clean fuel filter. Tighten all loose bolts, nuts, and connections in compartment.	Clean compartment. Operate and check floor drain valve.
	Drain sediment from fuel tanks.	Clean compartment. Clean and oil escape hatch.	

Tank Commander	Gunner	Bow Gunner	Driver
	Help perform 250-mile lubrication. Clean and touch-up any rust spots in turret.	Operate and check floor drain valve. Help perform 250-mile lubrication.	Dismount; open engine doors; clean engine and engine compartment; operate and check engine compartment drain valves. Perform 250-mile lubrication, referring to appropriate guide. Close engine doors.
Command REPORT.	Report "Gunner Ready".	Report "Bog Ready".	Report "Driver Ready".

40. RADIO. The tank commander will make the following inspection of radio sets (SCR-508, SCR-528, and SCR-538) prior to operation.

a. Cords. See that insulation and plugs are dry, unbroken, and making good contact. Arrange loose cordage to prevent its entangling personnel or equipment.

b. Antenna. See that

(1) Mast sections are tight. (Do not remove taped joints.)

(2) Leads at transmitter, receiver, and mast base are tight.

(3) Mast base is tight and not cracked.

(4) Insulators that pass through the armor plate and bulkheads are not broken or out of place.

c. Radio set mounting, snaps, snubbers, etc. Check for security and condition.

d. Microphones, switches, headsets. Check for condition and proper positions. Replace all defective headsets and microphones from spares and turn defective equipment in for repair or replacement.

e. Spare antenna sections. See that they are correctly placed in the roll and stowed to avoid being damaged.

f. Set grounding. Check connections.

g. Tubes. See that they are firmly seated in the sockets. Turn in the defective tubes at the earliest opportunity.

h. Fuses. Check condition, and spare supply for number and proper rating.

i. Cleanliness. See that radio sets and associated equipment are clean.

j. Battery voltage. Check with driver to see that the battery voltage is kept up. If voltage is low, have driver start the auxiliary generator. Always have generator running when radio is used and tank engine is not.

k. Crystals. Check for number, position, and frequency. Be sure required crystals are present.

Section X

SIGHT ADJUSTMENT

41. FIELD CHECK OF SIGHTS. Frequent checking of the sights is vital in the field. This is done by selecting a distant aiming point as explained in paragraph 42a, and aligning the crosshairs of the coaxial telescope on it. Then check to see whether the crosshairs of the periscopic telescope coincide on the same point. If they do, the sights are assumed to be still in adjustment. If they do not, the adjustment has slipped and a new adjustment for both sights must be made.

42. SIGHT ADJUSTMENT. Sights are in adjustment when the axis of the bore is parallel to the line of sighting of the telescope (and periscope). For practical purposes these lines are considered parallel when they converge on a point not less than 1500 yards distant.

a. Distant aiming point method. Select a point such as a building, telegraph pole, or smokestack at least 1500

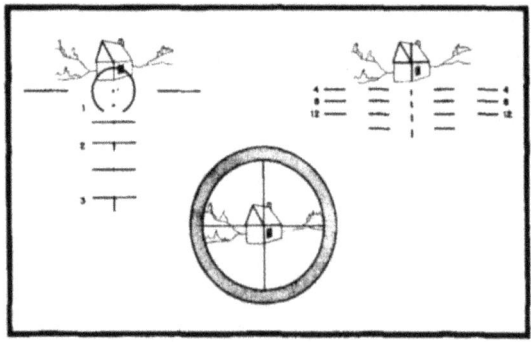

Figure 18. Sight adjustment on distant aiming point.

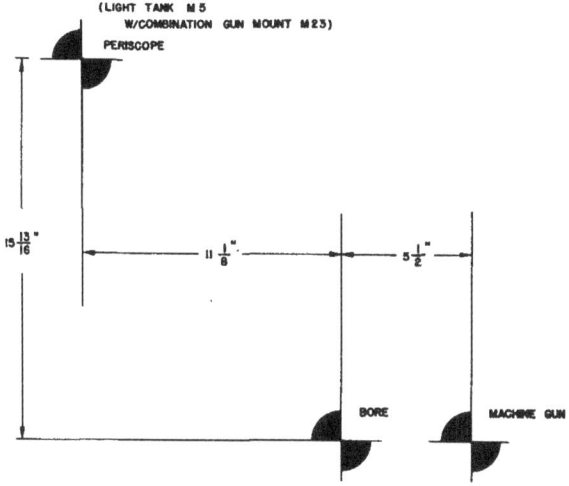

Figure 19. Testing target for combination gun mount M23.

yards away, preferably one having distinct vertical and horizontal straight lines which intersect, and thus render the alignment of the crosshairs easier and more accurate. Line the gun tube on this point, using the issue bore sights if they are available, or improvising crosshairs for the muzzle and sighting through the firing pin well of the closed breechblock. Then move both sights vertically and horizontally until their crosshairs coincide with the selected aiming point (figure 18). When there is a clamping device to secure this adjustment of the coaxial telescope once it is made, recheck after tightening to be sure that the adjustment has not been thrown off. Readings of the adjusting knob indices are recorded on all spare heads of the periscopic sights.

b. **Testing target.** When vision is limited by atmospheric conditions, close country, or jungle growth, the best field check for sighting equipment is the testing target, since it requires a clearing only 80 to 120 feet long. If issue testing targets are not available they may be constructed using the dimensions indicated for each gun mount in figures 19 and 20.

NOTE: Manufacturing variance frequently causes individual tanks to have dimensions varying widely from those used on the issue or constructed testing target. Therefore, the testing target must be carefully checked against the gun and sights which have been adjusted by the distant aiming point method on a clear day. Any discrepancies in dimensions will require that a separate testing target be constructed for use *only with that tank gun.*

The boresights are installed as in a, after which the crosshairs in the tube are aligned on the portion of the testing target marked "BORE". Without disturbing the gun, the sights are adjusted until the zero points in the reticles coincide with the intersection of the cross lines marked "PERISCOPE" and "TELESCOPE". Readings of the adjusting knob indices are recorded on all spare heads of the periscopic sights.

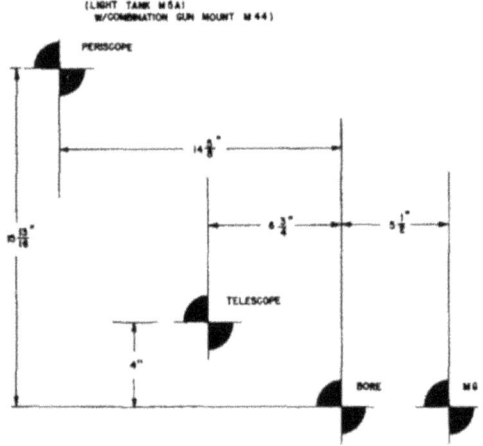

Figure 20. Testing target for combination gun mount M44.

Section XI

DESTRUCTION OF MATERIEL AND EQUIPMENT

43. GENERAL. a. The destruction of materiel is a command decision to be implemented only on authority delegated by the division or higher commander. This is usually made a matter of standing operating procedure. *It is ordered only after every possible measure for preservation or salvage of the materiel has been taken, and when in the judgment of the military commander concerned such action is necessary to prevent—*

(1) Its capture intact by the enemy.

(2) Its use by the enemy, if captured, against our own or allied troops.

(3) Its abandonment in the combat zone.

(4) Knowledge of its existence, functioning, or exact specifications from reaching enemy intelligence.

b. The principles followed are

(1) Methods for the destruction of materiel subject to capture or abandonment in the combat zone must be adequate, uniform, and easily followed in the field.

(2) Destruction is as complete as available time, equipment, and personnel permit. If thorough destruction of all parts cannot be completed, the most important features of the materiel are destroyed, and parts essential to the operation or use of the materiel and which cannot be easily duplicated, are ruined or destroyed. *The same essential parts are destroyed on all like units to prevent the enemy's constructing one complete unit from several damaged ones by "cannibalism".*

c. Crews are trained in the prescribed methods of destruction. *Training does not involve the actual destruction of materiel.*

d. Methods. (1) The methods below are given in order of effectiveness. If method No. 1 cannot be used, destruction is accomplished by one of the other methods outlined in order of priority shown. Adhere to the sequences.

(2) Certain methods require special tools and equipment such as TNT and incendiary grenades, which may not be items of issue normally. The issue of such special tools and materiel, the vehicles for which issued, and the conditions under which destruction will be effected are command decisions in each case, according to the tactical situation.

44. DESTRUCTION OF THE 37-MM GUN, TANK. a Remove the periscopic and telescopic sights. *If evacuation is possible, carry the sights.* If evacuation is not possible, thoroughly smash the sight and all spare sights.

b. Method No. 1. (1) Open drain plug on recoil mechanism, allowing recoil fluid to drain. It is not necessary to wait for the recoil fluid to drain completely before igniting the fuse in (5) below.

(2) Remove an HE shell from a complete round and seat the shell in the chamber.

(3) Plug the bore for approximately two-thirds of its length, using a rammer staff wrapped with cloth or waste to make it fit tightly in the bore. Mud, stones, clay, or other material may be used to plug the bore in lieu of the cleaning staff.

(4) Cut down a 1/2-pound TNT block to fit snugly in the chamber behind the HE shell. Insert a tetryl nonelectric cap into the TNT block with approximately 3 or 4 feet of safety fuse. Close the breech as far as possible without damaging the safety fuse.

(5) Ignite the safety fuse and take cover. Elapsed time: 2 or 3 minutes if rammer staff is used to plug the bore and the cut-down TNT block is carried with gun; longer if other bore obstructions are used.

c. **Method No. 2.** (1) See **b** (1) above.

(2) See **b** (3) above.

(3) Insert one complete HE round into gun and close breech.

(4) Take cover and fire the gun, using a cord. Elapsed time: 1 to 2 minutes using cleaning staff to plug the bore; longer if bore is plugged with mud, or other material.

d. **Method No. 3.** From point-blank range fire AP ammunition at the gun tube until it is rendered useless.

e. **Method No. 4.** (Elapsed time: 2 or 3 minutes.)

(1) See **b** (1) above.

(2) Fire one HE round against a similar round jammed in the muzzle. Take precautions prescribed in **c** (4) above.

45. DESTRUCTION OF THE GYRO-STABILIZER.

a. Drain oil from system.

b. Smash oil lines.

c. Smash control box.

d. Place an M14 incendiary grenade on control box and pull pin.

46. DESTRUCTION OF CALIBER .30 MACHINE GUN. a. Method No. 1. Field strip. Use barrel as a sledge. Raise cover and smash down toward front. Deform and break backplate; deform T-slot. Wedge lock frame, back down, into top of receiver between top plate and extractor cam; place chamber end of barrel over lock frame depressors and break off depressors. Insert barrel extension into back of receiver allowing the shank to protrude; knock off shank by striking with barrel from the side. Deform and crack receiver by striking with barrel at side plate corners nearest feedway. Elapsed time: 2-1/2 minutes.

b. **Method No. 2.** Insert bullet point of complete round into muzzle and bend case slightly, distending mouth of case to permit pulling of bullet. Spill powder from case, retaining sufficient powder to cover the bottom of case to a depth of approximately 1/8-inch. Reinsert pulled bullet, point first, into the case mouth. Load and fire this round with the reduced charge; the bullet will stick in the bore. Chamber one complete round, lay weapon on ground, and fire with a 30-foot cord. Use the best available cover as this means of destruction may be dangerous to the person destroying the weapon. Elapsed time: 2 to 3 minutes.

c. Small arms cannot be adequately damaged by firing with the barrel stuck in the ground, with or without a bullet jammed in the muzzle.

d. Machine gun tripod mount, calber .30 M2. Use machine gun barrel as a sledge. Deform traversing dial. Fold rear legs, turn mount over on head, stand on folded rear legs, knock off traversing dial locking screw, pintle lock, and deform head assembly. Deform folded rear legs so as to prevent unfolding. Extend elevating screw and bend screw by striking with barrel; bend pintle yoke. Elapsed time: 2 minutes.

47. DESTRUCTION OF THE LIGHT TANK, M5 SERIES. a. Method No. 1. (1) Remove and empty the portable fire extinguishers. Smash radio (see paragraph 50). Puncture fuel tanks. Use fire of caliber .50 machine gun, or a cannon, or use a fragmentation grenade for this purpose. Place TNT charges as follows:

(*a*) 3 pounds between engines.

(*b*) 2 pounds against left side of transfer unit as near differential as possible.

(*c*) One-half pound against left fuel tank. Use only a cap (no fuse) in this charge. Point cap end toward 3-pound charge. Insert tetryl nonelectric caps with at least 5 feet of safety fuse in each charge. Ignite the fuses and take cover. Elapsed time: 1 to 2 minutes if charges are prepared beforehand and carried in the vehicle.

(2) If sufficient time and materials are available, additional destruction of track-laying vehicles may be accomplished by placing a 2-pound TNT charge about the center of each track-laying assemblage. Detonate those charges in the same manner as the others.

(3) If charges are prepared beforehand and carried in the vehicle, keep the caps and fuses separated from the charges until used.

b. Method No. 2. Remove and empty the portable fire extinguishers. Smash radio. Puncture fuel tanks. Fire on the vehicle using adjacent tanks, antitank or other artillery, or antitank rockets or grenades. Aim at the engine, suspension, and armament in the order named. If a good fire is started, the vehicle may be considered destroyed. Elapsed time: About 5 minutes per vehicle. Destroy the last remaining vehicle by the best means available. Danger from cannibalism is inherent in this method.

48. DESTRUCTION OF AMMUNITION. a. General. Time will not usually permit the destruction of all ammunition in forward combat zones. When sufficient time and materials are available, ammunition is destroyed as indicated below. At least 30 to 60 minutes are required to destroy adequately the ammunition carried by combat units. In general, the methods and safety precautions outlined in TM 9-1900 are followed whenever possible.

b. Unpacked complete round ammunition. (1) Stack ammunition in small piles. (Small arms ammunition may be heaped.) Stack or pile most of the available gasoline in cans and drums around the ammunition. Throw onto the pile all available inflammable material, such as rags, scrap wood, and brush. Pour the remaining gasoline over the pile. Sufficient inflammable material is used to insure a very hot fire. Ignite the gasoline and take cover.

(2) 37-mm ammunition is destroyed by sympathetic detonation, using TNT. Stack ammunition in two stacks, about three inches apart, bases toward each other. Use

one pound of TNT to six or seven pounds of ammunition. From cover detonate all TNT charges simultaneously.

c. Packed complete round ammunition. (1) Stack the boxed ammunition in small piles. Cover with all available inflammable materials, such as rags, scrap wood, brush, and gasoline in drums or cans. Pour other gasoline over the pile. Ignite and take cover. (Small arms ammunition must be broken out of boxes or cartons before burning.)

(2) The destruction of packed complete round ammunition by sympathetic detonation with TNT is not advocated for use in forward combat zones. To insure satisfactory destruction involves putting TNT in alternate boxes of ammunition, a time-consuming job.

(3) In rear areas or fixed installations, sympathetic detonation may be used to destroy large ammunition supplies if destruction by burning is not feasible. Stack the boxes, placing in alternate boxes in each row sufficient TNT blocks to insure the use of one pound per six or seven rounds of 37-mm ammunition. Place the TNT blocks at the base end of the rounds. Detonate all TNT charges simultaneously. See FM 5-25 for details of demolition planning and procedure.

d. Miscellaneous. Grenades, antitank mines, and antitank rockets are destroyed by the methods outlined in **b** and **c** above for complete rounds. The amount of TNT necessary to detonate these munitions is considered less than that required for detonating artillery shells.

49. FIRE CONTROL EQUIPMENT. All fire control equipment including optical sights and binoculars, is difficult to replace. It is the last equipment to be destroyed, if there is any chance of personnel being able to evacuate. If evacuation of personnel is made, all possible items of fire control equipment are carried. If evacuation is impossible, fire control equipment is thoroughly destroyed by smashing and burying.

50. **DESTRUCTION OF RADIO EQUIPMENT.** a. **Books and papers.** Instruction books, circuit and wiring diagrams, records of all kinds for radio equipment, code books, and registered documents are destroyed by burning.

b. **Radio sets.** (1) Shear off all panel knobs, dials, etc., with an axe. Break open set compartment by smashing in the panel face, then knock off the top, bottom, and sides. The object is to destroy the panel and expose the chassis.

(2) On top of the chassis strike all tubes and circuit elements with the axe head. On the underside of the chassis, if it can be reached, use the axe to shear or tear off wires and small circuit units. Break sockets and cut unit and circuit wires. Smash or cut tubes, coils, crystal holders, microphones, earphones, and batteries. Break mast sections and break mast base at the insulator.

(3) When possible, pile up smashed equipment, pour on gas or oil and set it on fire. If other inflammable material, such as wood, is available, use it to increase fire effect. Bury smashed parts whether burned or not.

APPENDIX

REFERENCES

See FM 21-6, *List of Publications for Training*, and FM 21-7, *List of Training Film Strips, and Film Bulletins*, for full list of references.

FM 17-5	Armored Force Drill.
FM 17-12	Tank Gunnery.
FM 21-5	Military Training.
FM 23-40	Thompson Submachine Gun, Cal .45, M1928A1.
FM 23-41	Submachine Gun, Cal .45, M3.
FM 23-55	Browning Machine Gun, Cal .30.
TM 9-250	37-mm Tank Gun M6.
TM 9-732	Light Tanks M5 and M5A1.
TM 9-850	Cleaning, Preserving and Lubricating Materials.
TM 11-600	Radio Sets SCR-508, SCR-528, and SCR-538.

War Department Lubrication Order No. 81.

Preliminary Inspection for Radio Sets SCR-508, SCR-528, and SCR-538.

SNL G-103	Light Tank, M5 Series.
SNL K-1	Cleaning, Preserving, and Lubricating Materials.
SNL A-45	37-mm Gun M6.
Training Film 17-576	Tank Driving, Part II—Advanced.
Film Strip 2-18	Cavalry Weapons — Browning Machine Gun, Cal .30, M1919A4—Headspace Adjustment, Care and Cleaning, Mechanical Functioning.

Film Strip 7-60	Browning Machine Gun, Cal .30, HB, M1919A4 (Ground). Part I.
Film Strip 7-61	Browning Machine Gun, Cal .30, HB, M1919A4 (Ground). Part II.
Film Strip 7-63	Browning Machine Gun, Cal .30, M1917, Part VIII. Section I, Stoppages and Immediate Action.
Film Strip 17-2	Thompson Submachine Gun, Cal .45, M1928A1—Mechanical Training.
Film Strip 17-32	Cal .45 Submachine Gun, M3.

INDEX

	Paragraphs	Pages
Abandon tank	27	44
Action:		
Dismounted	24–29	37
In case of fire	26	43
Mounted	19–23	31
Advice to instructors	28	44
Ammunition:		
Destruction	48	75
Inspection before firing	20, 35	32, 52
Loading in tank	22	36
Auxiliary generator:		
To inspect	35	52
To start or stop	19, 21	31, 34
Breechblock:		
To close	15	19
To open	15	19
Crews:		
Composition	3	4
Control	5, 6	6, 8
Drill	7–12	10
Formations	4	5
To close and open hatches	9	13
To dismount	10	14
To form	7	10
To mount	8	11
Destruction of materiel	43–50	71
Dismounted action	24–29	37
Dismounting:		
Through escape hatch	11	15
Through hatches	10	14
Duties in firing	20, 23	32
Empty cases	21	34, 36
Equipment, destruction of	43–50	71
Escape hatch, to dismount through	11	15
Evacuation of casualties	30–33	46
Extinguishers, fire	26	43

	Paragraphs	Pages
Field check of sights	41	68
Fire:		
Engine	26	43
Hull	26	43
Fighting on foot	24, 25	37, 39
Firing:		
Duties of crew	20	32
To cease	21	34
Formations	4	5
Gun crew:		
Composition	13	19
Positions	4, 14	5, 19
Gun, 37-mm tank:		
Destruction	44	72
Firing	15	19
Immediate action	18	29
Inspections	35–39	52
Laying	15	19
Loading and unloading	15	19
Malfunctions and remedies	17	27
Operation	15	19
To secure	21	34
Immediate action	18	29
Inspections:		
After operation	38	63
At the halt	37	61
Before operation	35	52
During operation	36	60
Periodic additional services	39	64
Radio	40	67
Interphone operation	5, 6	6, 8
Maintenance after operation	38	63
Mounted action	19–23	31
Mounting through hatches	8	11
Muzzle covers	21, 35	34, 52
Operation of gun	15	19
Out of action	25	39
Park and bivouac precautions	29	45

	Paragraphs	Pages
Pep drill	12	17
Posts:		
Dismounted	4	5
Mounted	4	5
Prepare to fire	19	31
Purpose and scope	1	1
Radio:		
Destruction	50	77
Inspection	40	67
Operation	5	6
SCR-506	5	6
Ready rack, to refill	21, 22	34, 36
Safety precautions	16, 29	27, 45
Service of the piece	13–18	19
Sight adjustment	41, 42	68
Tank, destruction of	47	74
Turret control	6	8
Weapons:		
Destruction	27, 44, 46	44, 72, 73
Inspection	19, 35	31, 52
To load	23	36

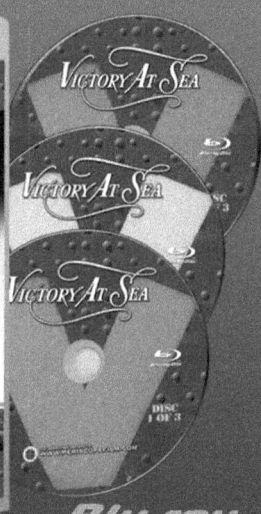

IN HIGH DEFINITION
NOW AVAILABLE!

COMPLETE LINE OF WWII AIRCRAFT FLIGHT MANUALS

WWW.PERISCOPEFILM.COM

©2011 PERISCOPE FILM LLC
ALL RIGHTS RESERVED
ISBN #978-1-935700-80-7
WWW.PERISCOPEFILM.COM

www.ingramcontent.com/pod-product-compliance
Lightning Source LLC
Chambersburg PA
CBHW070653050426
42451CB00008B/332